Norse Mythology

A Guide to Norse Gods, Mythology, and Folklore

Ross Romano

Table of Contents

The Origin Story 1

Chapter 1: The Nine Realms 5

Chapter 2: Gods, Goddesses, and Creatures of the Nine Realms 17

Chapter 3: The Monsters of the Nine Realms 39

Chapter 4: A Hero's Tale 47

The End 58

The Origin Story

In every tale ever told there is a beginning as well as an end. In Norse mythology, the beginning of the universe is as important as the creation of its tales, myths, and legends. The origin of the nine realms starts with Ginnungagap.

Ginnungagap was a bottomless pit of nothing. In this darkness and silence, life was created with the help of fire and ice. Far to the sides of the Ginnungagap were the lands Muspelheim and Niflheim. Muspelheim was a hot and fiery place while Niflheim was a cold, icy place.

These two places started to rise in power and compete with each other. Eventually, they clashed in the Ginnungagap. The fire melted the ice and formed drops of water. From within the hissing and the sputtering, the drops of water clumped together to form Ymir who was the first creation in the Ginnungagap. Ymir, which means Screamer, was the first of the frost giants. The frost giants were godlike, but cruel and destructive.

From Ymir came the start of creation. He was a hermaphrodite and when he slept, giants formed from his legs and from the sweat from his armpit. This was the start of the giant race.

The frost continued to melt and from it formed a cow, Audhumla. Ymir was nourished by her milk and she kept herself alive and strong by licking the salt in the ice. As Audhumla continued to lick away at the ice, she slowly uncovered Buri who was hidden there. Buri was the first of the tribe of gods known as the Aesir. From Buri came her son, Bor, who then married Bestla, who was the daughter of one of the giants.

Bor and Bestla had three children who were the first of the half-giant half-god race. Their names were Vili, Ve, and Odin. Odin would later become the chief of the Aesir gods, but first, he and his two brothers set about constructing the world.

Odin and his brothers saw the giants' violent cruel nature, most of all Ymir, and they slew him. From his body, they set to work constructing the world. His blood spilled along the ground and formed into the oceans. They took his skin and muscles and formed them into the soil for the ground. They used his hair to create vegetation, and his brains became the clouds. Four dwarves stood on each corner of the world, holding up a part of the Ymir's skull above the earth to create the sky. These four points then became North, South, East, and West.

Odin, Vili, and Ve created the world and, eventually, they created the first humans. One day, Odin and his two brothers were walking along the coast of one of the lands they created when they came across two pieces of wood. They were shaped like people, but they were lifeless, and so the three gods decided to give them what they did not have.

Odin breathed life into them while his brothers gave them creativity and thinking, as well as the ability to see, hear, taste, touch, smell, and speak. They dressed them and named them Ash and Embla. Odin then gave them Midgard as their dwelling place and built a fence around it so they would be protected from the giants. Ash and Embla were the first male and female, and they later became the father and mother of the entire human civilization.

In the beginning, there was nothingness. Ginnungagap was the very embodiment of chaos. It was a void. There was nothing there and yet it still contained everything the gods needed to create the world. Ymir was the first to be created from this chaos and it seems only poetic that he be the building blocks of the world. The Ginnungagap used what it had to create Ymir, and the gods used Ymir to create the world we know today.

Throughout Norse mythology, giants continue to play the same role as Ymir. They are not only mindless, destructive creatures. They act as the building blocks of chaos and creation. In the beginning, there was no order, the gods had to create that. So, it makes sense that the giants work hard to destroy and corrupt that created order because they are still the embodiment of formless chaos.

In Norse mythology, you can see that both gods and giants play an important role in creation. The gods created the world as we know it and they helped shape it. They continued to intervene in the world's affairs, keeping a steady hand on its development until the end. However, it is also seen that the world is what it is due to the influence of the giants. The world was created from Ymir's body, so if it was not for the giants, there would still be nothing. Ginnungagap would continue to be an endless void.

The world is held together by the constant struggle between the gods and the giants. On one side there is order, holiness, and goodness. On the other side, there is chaos, profaneness, and wickedness. The gods and giants embody these traits, and their constant struggle makes up the world. The tension has always been there since the beginning and it will remain until Ragnarok. This will be the end of everything. When the world is destroyed, the constant struggle will finally cease, and everything will return to the way it was before. There will once again be only Ginnungagap and it will contain only darkness, silence, and nothing.

According to Norse mythology, until Ragnarok arrives, the world will continue this way and the gods will continue to shape it the way they see fit. They created the world, and within that world, the nine realms will thrive.

Chapter 1: The Nine Realms

The cosmos in Norse mythology is a collection of realms all held up and connected by one great tree. You could say that all the worlds exist in different spiritual realms, but they sometimes overlap throughout the Norse stories. The gods could travel between realms as they pleased, but others could not.

The nine realms rest on the large trunk, strong branches, and old roots of the great ash tree. They are named as follows:

Asgard

Alfheim

Vanaheim

Midgard

Muspelheim

Niflheim

Jotunheim

Svartalfaheim

Helheim

Before we look into each of the nine realms, we must first understand the great ash tree that holds them all up.

Yggdrasil

The great ash tree known as Yggdrasil exists in the Ginnungagap. Its large, strong branches reach high into the heavens. It has three great roots, each of which extend downward and feed from three separate wells. The first well is known as the Well of Urda, and it is where the gods hold their daily council. The second well is known as Hvergelmir, and it is more of a stream than a well. The third and final well is called Mimisbrunnr, after the wise being, Mimir, that protects it.

There are three female entities that are known as the Norns. They spin the threads of fate which control the lives of everyone. One of the three draws the thread of life, another, measures it to decide how long that life will be, and the third cuts the thread when that life has come to an end. The Norns dwell near the well of Urda, and they pour the water from the well over Yggdrasil. The exact location of Urda's well and the three Norns is unknown. It is said that it can be found in Asgard itself and that the root of Yggdrasil grows up into the heavens in order to reach it. This would make sense if the Aesir Gods use it as the place for their daily council, but it is unclear if this is the true location of the well.

There are four stags known as Dvalinn, Dainn, Durapror, and Duneyrr that continuously feed on the leaves of Yggdrasil, but the tree is kept healthy and evergreen. It always heals itself so it can nourish the aggressive nature of life.

Around the base of the great tree lives Nidhogg, the great dragon. Nidhogg is always gnawing at the roots of Yggdrasil and it is said that one day he will eventually gnaw through one of the roots, destabilizing the great tree and bringing about Ragnarok.

At the very top of the tree sits a great eagle that is nameless. This great eagle is said to hate the dragon Nidhogg, and vice versa. A squirrel, named Ratatoskr, takes joy in their hatred for each other and so he runs up and down the trunk of Yggdrasil delivering messages of insults and hatred from Nighogg to the eagle and from the eagle to Nidhogg. It takes the squirrel a whole day to run from the top of the great ash tree to the base, but he enjoys this task too much to care. Sometimes the squirrel delivers fake messages just for fun so he can watch the two of them fight.

Yggdrasil is the world tree that stands tall and mighty in the very center of the universe. Its branches reach high up into the heavens and its roots reach deep down into the underworld. It is the very fabric of the universe and a symbol of mortality. Although it is strong and evergreen, it has many creatures constantly gnawing and biting at it.

Nobody knows just how Yggdrasil came to be; it has always been there.

Asgard

Asgard is the home of the Aesir Gods and is the highest realm on the world tree. It is said to be the most fertile and lively of all the domains. There are plants of all kinds growing everywhere and the buildings themselves are said to be made of gold. It is the most abundant, colorful, and grand realm of the nine.

The highest of the gods live in this realm, including Thor, Frigg, and Odin himself. Odin sits on a high throne at the very top of Asgard, from which he is always watching. He watches all the nine realms with the help of his crows, and he defends the realms with the help of his wolves.

Asgard is also home to the largest hall of them all, known as Valhalla, which when translated means "hall of the slain." Valhalla is a large feasting hall with a long table stretching from one end to the other. The table is always filled with food and drink and there are plenty of seats for those who come there. Only great warriors who have fallen in battle are allowed to join the feast in this hall. Odin chooses these warriors himself, depending on how bravely they fought in battle. It is said that you can only be chosen for Valhalla if you have died during combat.

The warriors who Odin has chosen, wait in Valhalla, eating, drinking, dancing, and enjoying their time. However, they also train and prepare themselves for a greater battle yet to come.

Odin has chosen the greatest warriors to join him in this hall so they can fight beside him in the final battle at Ragnarok.

Asgard is surrounded by a high, strong, and incomplete wall. Odin asked that the wall be built in order to protect Asgard from the growing strength and hatred of the giants, but Thor was forced to kill its builder before its completion.

Alfheim

Alfheim is next on the world tree. Alfheim roughly translates into "Elfland" or "Land of the Elves." Not much is known of this realm except for what you can gather from the name. It is the realm where the light elves live, and it is said to be the original home of the Goddess, Freya. Freya is now in Asgard with the Aesir Gods and she does not speak much of her home in Alfheim.

The God Freyr is the ruler in Alfheim and the elves are known as minor gods representing both nature and fertility. They are also known as guardian angels. They have the power to either hinder or help humans using their magical powers or their knowledge.

There are not many tales or poems mentioning this realm and how it looks, although the elves themselves are described as being more beautiful than the sun. It is suggested, given the elves' appearance and culture, that Alfheim is a green and abundant land, filled with sun, warmth, and plant life.

Vanaheim

It is not clear where exactly on the world tree Vanaheim is located, but it is safe to say that it is somewhere near the top near Asgard. Just like the land of the light elves, not much is known about Vanaheim or how it looks.

Vanaheim is home to a group of gods known as the Vanir Gods. They are an old branch of gods and a lot smaller in numbers and power compared to the Aesir Gods. They were mostly known for their sorcery and magic as they were masters of it. Vanir Gods are also known for their sight and ability to see into the future.

A long time ago, there was a war between the Vanir Gods and the Aesir Gods. It was a war that raged on for years and it seemed never-ending. Both sides were strong and powerful, able to heal and adapt from any attack. Like everything else, the war eventually came to an end with the Aesir Gods rising to the top.

After the war, Njord, Freyr, and Freya who were originally Vanir Gods moved to Asgard to live there as a token of peace.

Midgard

Midgard can be found in the center of the world tree, directly beneath Asgard. It is the home of the humans and its name can be translated into the term, "middle earth." Midgard and Asgard are connected via the Bifrost, which is a rainbow bridge that the gods use to travel between the two realms. Only a god can use this bridge, and it is solely controlled by Odin.

Midgard is surrounded by a large, never-ending ocean. It is said that the ocean cannot be passed. The ocean is home to a large sea serpent known as the Midgard Serpent, and it guards the realm and its inhabitants from any who might try and pass through the ocean. It is believed that the serpent is so large that it encompasses the whole world.

Muspelheim

This was one of the first realms to come into existence. It was created at the same time as Niflheim, but as its complete opposite. Muspelheim was created far to the south of the universe, and it is known as the land of fire. It is a hot place that is constantly burning. It is filled with lava, flames, fire, sparks, and soot. If you think that this land would be barren and lifeless, then you would be wrong.

Muspelheim is home to many creatures, most of which thrive in the extreme heat and the darkness. Fire demons and fire giants live in this realm and they are ruled by an enormous giant called Surtr.

Muspelheim is one of the most important realms in existence as it was a key ingredient in the creation of life within the Ginnungagap.

Niflheim

Niflheim was one of the two realms to first exist within the universe. Its icy winds were essential for creating the first life of the universe, but there are other ways in which it is still very important.

It is a dark and cold place, the darkest and coldest realm out of the nine, and it is known as the home of fog and mist. The oldest spring in existence is located here and it is called Hvergelmir. It is one of the three wells that feed the three roots of Yggdrasil. It is said that, in the beginning, when the world tree first began to grow, it stretched one of its roots far into Niflheim and fed on the spring to keep itself strong.

This spring is guarded by Nidhogg, and this is also the root that he constantly gnaws on.

Legends of the spring say that all cold rivers in the universe flow from it, and that it is the source of the eleven rivers that flow throughout the universe. Many stories are told of the spring, but legend says that it is the origin of all living things and it is the place where all living things will go back to.

Jotunheim

This realm is known as the home of the giants, enemies of the Aesir Gods. More specifically, it is home to both the frost giants and the rock giants. It is located near the bottom of the world tree, by its roots. In Jotunheim, the terrain is rocky and filled with dense forests. The land here is not fertile, therefore the giants cannot grow anything. Due to this, they solely live off of the fish from the water, and the animals from the forests. Jotunheim is also known as a snowy place. It is kept separate from Asgard by a large river called Iving that never freezes over, no matter how cold it is.

The giants and the Aesir Gods are constantly fighting, although there have been some instances of love affairs between the two. Loki himself comes from Jotunheim, but he was accepted by the Aesir Gods as one of them.

Jotunheim has a stronghold known as Utgard, their version of Asgard, and it is said to be so tall that no one can see to the top. It was carved out of the snow and ice, and only one giant lives inside. He is Utgard-Loki, the feared King of Jotunheim.

This realm is also home to the second well and the second root of the world tree. Mimisbrunnr, also known as Mimir's Well, is the well of wisdom and is protected by the wise Mimir and his children. Mimir is the wisest of all the Gods and knows many secrets and hidden knowledge given to him by the well. Mimir drinks from the well every day and it gives him superior wisdom and knowledge. This is his reward from presiding over the well and protecting Yggdrasil's great roots.

Svartalfheim

This realm is also found near the bottom of the world tree, by its roots, and it is the home of the dwarves. It is said to be a dark place that is mostly rocky and barren. This tales suggest that this is actually the home of the dark elves instead of being home to the dwarves. It is still unclear which race lives in Svartalfheim.

What is clear is that either the dwarves, or dark elves, live underground in caves and tunnels. The dwarves seldom come up to the surface. They are also famous for being master craftsmen, and they have made many powerful gifts for the Aesir Gods. Draupnir, the magical ring, and Gungni, Odin's powerful spear, are a few of the notable gifts they have made for the gods.

Helheim

Hel, also called Helheim, is the lowest realm on the world tree. It sits at the base of the tree's roots, directly in the center. It is the underworld and is the home for the dishonorable dead. Murderers, thieves, and those who are not considered to be brave enough to live in Valhalla or Falkvangr are the dishonorable dead that are sent to Hel.

This realm is very dark, cold, and lifeless. It is said that this place is not an end to life, but rather, a bleak continuation of it. All who go to this realm will never feel happiness or joy again. It is ruled over by the goddess, Hel. The realm is named for her, not the other way around.

Hel is not known to be worse or better than life. It is not seen as a punishment for doing wrong or a reward for doing good. It is simply seen as life after death. Those who go to Hel will do anything that they would do if they were still alive. They would fight, play, eat, sleep, and so on. It is nothing like the forms of hell seen in most other religions.

It is said that there is only one way to get to Hel and that is to walk down a path. The path is long, wide, and shrouded in darkness. Those who go to Hel must walk in the pitch black. This path leads to a river named Gjoll, one of the eleven rivers that flow from Niflheim throughout the universe. This river flows in front of the entrance to Hel, which is a bridge. On the bridge stands a giantess who is the guardian of the bridge, and she will only let the dead pass over the bridge into Hel. If you are living, she will know, and she will ask you what your purpose in the land of the dead is. Depending on your answer, she will then decide to either let you pass into Hel or send you back along the path.

Hel is surrounded by a large wall with a great gate as an entrance. After crossing the bridge, the dead walk through the gate into Hel, but the living may never pass through this gate. In order to enter Hel, they must find a way over or around the wall, or else they have to turn back and leave the way they came.

Those are the nine realms and the great world tree, Yggdrasil, which make up the universe. They are all connected, while also existing by themselves. Without the great world tree, none of these realms would be able to exist within the Ginnungagap.

Chapter 2: Gods, Goddesses, and Creatures of the Nine Realms

The Gods in Norse mythology belong to two major groups, the Aesir, and the Vanir, but they are all gods in their own right. There are also some gods and goddesses that exist outside of these two groups. Each group has its higher gods that are more powerful and worshipped above others, and the lower gods that are still powerful but seen as weak in the eyes of the higher gods.

The only difference between the higher gods and the lesser gods is the role they play in Norse mythology. Some play larger roles in tales of bravery, cunning, wisdom, and battle, whereas others do not appear in tales at all.

The Higher Gods and Goddesses

Odin

Also known as the "All-Father," Odin is the most powerful and highest god in the universe. He is part of the group of Aesir Gods and was one of the first of the gods to exist. He is the ruler of Asgard and the protector of all the nine realms. Odin especially watches over Midgard, home to the humans, as he is one of the gods that created the humans and their home.

Odin is known as the God of War, the God of Poetry, and the God of Magic. He is also known to be paradoxical. He is a fearful god as well as simultaneously being a caring and loving god.

Odin is on a constant search for knowledge with the help of his two crows that fly over the nine realms, seeing all. They fly back to Asgard and sit on his shoulder, whispering the things they have seen into his ear. His two wolves run from one realm to another seeking out secrets to bring back to him. He also has the Valkyries, a collection of female warriors that also aid him in his never-ending search for knowledge and power.

Odin is most famous for sacrificing one of his eyes in order to see the universe more clearly, and for hanging himself from the tree of Yggdrasil in order to learn the secret runic alphabet. His thirst for knowledge is what makes him the most powerful, feared, and loved god of all the other gods, both Aesir and Vanir.

Frigg

She is Odin's wife and the goddess of fertility, love, fate, and beauty. She is also a symbol of all of these things. She is said to be the most beautiful goddess of all the Aesir and Vanir.

Frigg is a mighty queen among the gods, and the only one allowed to sit beside her husband, Odin. She is also very protective of her sons and is a great and loving mother. She went so far as to take an oath from all things in the universe, making them vow never to hurt her son, Balder.

Frigg is mostly known for her gift of sight. Although she can see into the future, she is surrounded by secrecy. Frigg is a beautiful, loving, and trusting queen, but her trust would eventually be betrayed by Loki.

Thor

Thor is the most well-known god, and son of Odin. He is an Aesir God that resides in Asgard and is the protector of humans and Midgard. He is also known as the God of Thunder and is a mighty warrior.

He wields a hammer called Mjolnir, which is the most powerful weapon in existence, and only he can wield it. It was said that his unique hammer is so powerful that it could slay giants and destroy mountains.

Thor is one of the most popular gods and also the strongest. He is so strong that not only is he entrusted to guard Midgard, but it is also his duty to guard Asgard, the stronghold of the Aesir.

Aside from his strength, Thor is also known for his healing powers, extreme bravery, righteousness, and bright red hair.

Loki

Loki, who is also known as the God of mischief, is not very strong or powerful compared to gods like Thor and Odin. He is not great in battle, nor would he win in a direct fight with many of the gods, but despite this, he is still responsible, directly or indirectly, for the death of many strong and powerful gods.

Loki is a wise trickster. He can think on his feet and he is always quick with an answer to any problem. He likes seeking out trouble, as is his nature. He originally lived in Jotunheim with the giants, but he was accepted by Odin and the other gods for several good deeds and was welcomed as an Aesir into Asgard. Odin considered Loki to be his brother. When Loki did something to anger Odin or the other gods, he was quick to appease them with a good deed or a gift of some kind.

One of Loki's most famous talents is his ability to shapeshift. This ability led to him fathering many monstrous and powerful children, one of which was the goddess, Hel.

Balder

Balder is the son of Frigg and Odin. He is described as being the very epitome of beauty, radiance, fairness, and kindness. According to legend, he is living between heaven and earth.

Balder is one of the most famous of gods for two reasons. First, he was the half-brother of the mighty Thor. Two, he is said to be immortal. Balder had a dream of his death, and as a result, lived his life in fear. His mother, Frigg, took it upon herself to see that her son would never die. She took an oath from everything in the universe that they would not harm her son. Balder lived through life winning every battle and boasting about his immortality to the point where he dared the Gods to try and kill him.

Despite his mother's best efforts to keep him safe, eventually, through the actions of Loki, he was killed.

Tyr

Tyr is a famous god, but he is also the lesser-known god of war. He is said to be an extremely strong god and a great warrior. He won many battles, most of which he fought with only one arm. He lost his other arm to Fenrir, the giant wolf, who is also one of Loki's many monstrous children.

He was a close friend of Odin and was beloved by many of the other gods.

Freya

Freya is often mistaken for the Goddess Frigg since they both represent the same ideals, but they are very different goddesses. Freya is associated with the same qualities as Frigg such as fertility, love, and beauty. However, Freya is the most beautiful of all the Aesir and Vanir, even more so than Frigg.

Freya does not have the gift of sight as Frigg does and she never married Odin. This is only one of the many differences between Frigg and Freya. Freya was the sister of Freyr. They were both Vanir that lived in Alfheim, land of the elves, but after the war between the Aesir and the Vanir, Freya went to live in Asgard as a token of peace.

Heimdall

Heimdall is most famous for being known as the shiniest of all the Vanir and the Aesir. His skin was so white that it glowed brightly like a star. Heimdall is also famous for being one of the sons of Odin with a most important task. He sat on top of the Bifrost, the bridge connecting the realm of Asgard to the realm of Midgard, and it was his job to protect it. No one walked over the bridge, for he was ever watchful and forever alert. It was his duty to keep Asgard safe from attack and to make sure the Bifrost was always a safe means of travel for the gods.

Vidar

Vidar is yet another of Odin's many sons. He is a very powerful god, more powerful than any other man or god besides Thor. His mother is a giantess named Grid, and his power and strength are only matched by Thor. Vidar is not a very famous god and had few accomplishments. He was mostly known for being the son of Odin and for killing the giant wolf, Fenrir, thus proving his strength.

Vidar is also considered by some to be the silent god of vengeance.

Vali

Vali is another half-brother of Thor, his father being Odin and his mother being unknown. He also proved himself to be very strong and powerful. It is said that his main purpose for being born was to kill his half-brother, Hodr, for killing his other half-brother, Balder. To do this, he needed a lot of strength. Vali ended up being so strong that in some versions of the story, he is one of the few gods that actually survived Ragnarok.

Hel

Hel is the Goddess of Helheim, the world of the undead that is named after her. It is said that when she is in her realm, she is even more powerful than Odin himself. She is the daughter of Loki and a giantess. This makes her a terrifying and strong individual.

It is said that her skin is pale and appears to be decaying. The gods found her not long after her birth, and when they saw how disgusting she was, they threw her down into the underworld. This is where she created and ruled her own realm, Helheim.

She is not a harsh and cruel ruler in her realm. She nurtures and cares for all who enter.

Elli

Elli is not a well-known goddess, but she is a very powerful one. She is the goddess of old age, and to signify this she often takes the appearance of an old woman. However, this appearance is a deceiving one. She is in fact, a capable and strong warrior. She even defeated Thor himself in a wrestling match, proving the strength that she is possesses, despite her appearance.

Freyr

Freyr is known for many things. He was the ruler of Alfheim, brother to Freya, and a very strong and wise Vanir. He is the god of fertility and is also seen as a symbol for prosperity. Freyr was once a ruler of Alfheim and a great warrior for the Vanir Gods until after the war between the Aesir and Vanir. He then went to Asgard to live there as a token of peace, alongside his sister.

The Lesser Gods and Goddesses

Borr

He is the father of the "All-Father" Odin and his two brothers, Vili and Ve.

Eir

She is the goddess of healing.

Delling

He is the god of dawn.

Dagur

He is the god of daytime, and the son of Nott and Delling.

Eostre

She is the goddess of Spring.

Forseti

He is the god of peace, justice, and truth, and is the son of Nanna and Balder.

Lofn

She is the goddess of forbidden love.

Bragi

He is the god of music, poetry, and the harp.

Gefjun

She is the goddess of the plow and of fertility.

Iounn

She is the goddess of youth.

Hlin

She is the goddess of protection and consolation.

Magni

He is the god of strength and is the son of Thor.

Nanna

She is the goddess of peace and joy and she is married to Odin's son, Balder. She mothered Forseti and died due to grief up the death of her husband, Balder.

Joro

She is the goddess of Earth.

Mani

He is the god of the moon.

Kvasir

He is the god of inspiration and is eventually killed by dwarves.

Njordur

She is the goddess of the fish, wind, sea, and wealth. She dies during Ragnarok.

Saga

She is the goddess of wisdom.

Nott

She is the goddess of the night and the mother of Jord, Aud, and Dagur.

Sif

She is the goddess of the harvest and she is married to Thor.

Ran

She is the goddess of the sea.

Thruer

She is the daughter of Thor and Sif.

Sigyn

She is the goddess of fidelity and is the wife of Loki.

Ullr

He is the god of winter, the hunt, and of dueling. He is also the son of Sif.

Sol

She is the goddess of the sun and she is eaten by Skoll at Ragnarok.

Sjofn

She is the goddess of love.

Var

She is the goddess of the contract.

Skadi

She is the goddess of the wilderness and she is Njordr's wife.

Vor

She is the goddess of wisdom.

Ve

He is one of the three gods of creations, and he is brother to Odin and Vili.

Vili

He is one of the three gods of creation, and he is brother to Odin and Ve.

Yggdrasil

She is known as the goddess of life and is the tree of life that connects all nine realms together.

Creatures of the Nine Realms

In Norse mythology, there are many creatures that can be described as neither gods nor monsters. They are simply creatures that live within the nine realms. Some live in peace, while others, seek out war and destruction.

Audhumbla

She is the first creature to exist in the world. She is a giant cow that was born from the same ice that bred the first giant, Ymir. She survived by licking the salt off of the ice, and Ymir survived by drinking her milk. They sustained each other and they were both essential to the existence of further life in the universe.

Arvak and Alsvid

In Norse mythology, these are the two celestial horses that pulled the chariot of Sol, goddess of the sun. Alsvid means "all swift" and Arvak means "early awake." They pull the chariot that carries a big ball of fire they fetched from Muspelheim. This is the sun that provides heat for the world, but it emits no light. The light we see in the sky comes from the horses' glowing manes.

Blodughofi

This is the horse of the god, Freyr. His name can be translated to mean "bloody hoof." He is a loyal and strong horse that carried Freyr wherever he needed to go. It is said that when Freyr fell in love with a woman from Jotunheim that he sent his servant there with a proposal of marriage. His servant rode there on Bludoghofi so he could ride past the wall of fire surrounding Jotunheim without being harmed.

Geri and Freki

These are the names of the wolves that sit beside Odin at the foot of his throne. Freki means "overeating" and Geri means "edacity." Odin did not eat, and so when he sat in the Hall of Valhalla, they would sit underneath the table by his feet and wait for him to drop food for them while he drank his mead.

Hrimfaxi

This is the celestial horse of Nott, the goddess of the night. Its name can be translated into either "frost mane" or "rime mane." Hrimfaxi would pull a black chariot carrying Nott across the sky at the end of the day, and when they appeared in the sky, a curtain of night would fall on the earth.

Gullfaxi

This is a celestial horse that changed hands from a giant named Hrungnir, to Thor's son, Magni. One day, the giant saw Odin riding his eight-legged horse and challenged him to a horse race. Odin won, but he and the gods still treated the giant to a drink.

While drinking, the giant got drunk and began to talk in ways that enraged Thor. Thor challenged him to a battle the next day. Thor won, killing the giant, but he was pinned underneath the giant's massive body. His son, Magni, who had only just been born three days prior to this battle, lifted the giant's body off of his father. Thor then rewarded his son with the giant's horse, Gullfaxi.

Grani

Grani is said to be a celestial horse that belonged to the goddess Sigurd, and was the descendent of the horse, Sleipnir.

Fialar and Gullinkambi

These are two cocks that would crow to one another. Gullinkambi sat in Asgard and his name means "golden comb." Gullinkambi would start to crow and Fialar would crow back. This would be a warning to all that Ragnarok was coming.

Heidrun

Hiedrun is a celestial goat that provided the souls of the dead that assemble at Valhalla with an endless supply of mead. Heidrun would feed on the leaves of the tree of life and mead would flow from its breasts. It kept the souls of the dead in Valhalla entertained and well supplied until the day of Ragnarok.

Sleipnir

This is Odin's trusted eight-legged horse, and another one of Loki's children. He is the son of a stallion named Svadilfari, and Loki, who had shaped shifted into a mare in order to distract the stallion. Loki gifted Sleipnir to Odin in order to appease him and seek forgiveness for his wrongdoings.

It is said that Sleipnir was the strongest and fastest of all the horses, and even rode one of the gods into Hel itself.

Hofvarpnir

This is a celestial horse that belonged to Frigg's maid, Gna. This horse could freely ride through the air and across the water.

Muninn and Huginn

These are the two crows or ravens that sat on each of Odin's shoulders. Muninn means "memory" and Huginn means "idea."

Their job was to seek knowledge and information for Odin who was always thirsty for it. They would fly from his shoulders at dawn and go to Midgard, the human world. There, they would see and hear all they could, and then, return to him at dusk.

They are often seen sitting on his shoulders and whispering all that they have learned in his ears. This is why Odin is sometimes referred to as the god of the raven.

Svadilfari

This is a celestial horse that belonged to a giant from Jotunheim, whose name is unknown. The meaning of the horse's name is unclear, although some think it means "slave" or "unlucky traveler." Odin's eight-legged horse, Sleipnir, is his descendant.

When the world had only just begun and the gods of Asgard wanted a wall built around their stronghold, Svadilfari and his master were tasked with building that wall. Svadilfari would help his master do this because he was a strong and powerful horse that could pull and transport large rocks with ease.

Gullinborsti

This name means "golden mane" or "golden boar." He is a celestial boar belonging to the god, Freyr. Gullinborsti is used to pull Freyr's chariot, and it was said that he could run over water and land faster than any horse could. This boar was fashioned for Freyr by the dwarves, and his golden mane is meant to represent either the maturation of the crops or the golden sunlight.

Valkyries

Valkyries could be considered creatures instead of gods or goddesses because they were technically spirits. They were a group of female spirits that helped Odin ferry the slain he had chosen to Valhalla.

Their name, which means "choosers of the slain", depicts that they do a lot more than just carrying the slain to Valhalla. The Valkyries' job is to choose who lives and dies in battle and then carry those who died honorably to the halls where they sit and await Ragnarok.

Dwarves

Svartalfheim, or the home of the black elves, is the realm where the dwarves live. In most depictions of dwarves, they are stout and short. However, there is no evidence in Norse mythology of this being true. They are considered to be lesser beings, and this might have made people believe them to be shorter than other higher beings.

Dwarves are very talented at smithing, mining, forging, and making things of great power and magic. It is said that they live underground in a complex labyrinth of caves, tunnels, and mines.

The dwarves' home is dry, dark, and barren, but somehow, they managed to survive and thrive underground. They have used their talents to make many powerful gifts and weapons for the gods. The most famous of these is Mjollnir, Thor's hammer.

Elves

Elves live in the realm, Alfheim, and they were thought to be demigods. However, this is not an entirely accurate description of them. Demigods are half-god and half-human, or at least a human with the strength and/or power of a god. The elves are neither of these. They are simply creatures that cannot be described as either god or human.

It is said that they are tall and slender with pale long hair and pale skin that almost glowed, and they are the most beautiful of all the creatures in the nine realms. The elves are said to be more beautiful than the sun, but not much is actually known about them or their realm. They are very secretive creatures that keep mostly to themselves.

They tend to keep clear of humans and the human world and, according to myth, they only appear to either cure an illness or cause it. This was, of course, dependent on that particular elf's whim. They have much power, but they are neither good nor evil.

They stood somewhere in between, capable of either helping or hurting humans depending on how they felt that day.

In some stories, elves are split into two groups, the dark elves and the light elves. Dark elves are meant to have pitch black skin, while the light elves are known to have skin lighter than the sun. It is unclear whether the elves are actually separated into these two groups. This could be a method by which humans describe the way elves could be either good or evil, or perhaps the dark elves were actually just dwarves under another name. Either way, it is clear that elves sit in a category of their own.

Jotnar

The Jotnar or for singular use, Jotunn, are creatures from Jotunheim. Most depictions of creatures from Jotunheim are shown to be giants of some kind, but there are other creatures that come from Jotunheim that fit into this category.

The Jotnar are often said to be at war with the Aesir and Vanir gods. However, many Norse gods are descendants of one or more Jotunn. Trolls are a subgroup of Jotnar, but they don't appear much in Norse mythology.

Some of the most famous Jotnar are Hel and Ymir.

Ratatoskr

He is the squirrel that runs up and down Yggdrasil, delivering messages from the dragon Nidhogg at the base of the tree to the great eagle at the top. Its name means either "drill-tooth" or "bore-tooth."

This squirrel is seen as playing an important role in the circle of life. The messages it delivers grow the hatred between the dragon and the eagle. Their hatred leads them both to attack the tree, which then leads to a cycle of decay that will eventually end in the rebirth of the tree.

Verdrfolnir

This is the great eagle that sits atop the world tree, Yggdrasil. It is unclear whether this is the eagle's true name or not. In some stories of the great eagle, he remains nameless, and in other stories, this is the name he is given.

He sits at the top of the tree and, when he beats his wings, he sends strong winds down through the nine realms. He hates the dragon that lives at the base of the tree and would often fly down there to attack him if he received a message from Ratatoskr that was vicious enough.

Chapter 3: The Monsters of the Nine Realms

Every story has its monsters. These are terrifying creatures meant to keep you up at night and trick naughty children into behaving. In Norse mythology, every living creature plays a vital role in the flow of the universe and in Ragnarok, especially the monsters. There are many monsters in the nine realms, and here we will discuss the fiercest and most evil of them all.

Draugr

Draugr are perhaps the most terrifying monsters of the nine realms. They are, simply put, the undead. It is said that the Draugr have superhuman strength, are able to shapeshift into any creature, and can increase their size at will. They are shrouded in the stench of decay and will walk the earth for few reasons. Draugr are also capable of swimming or walking straight through solid rock, which is how they are able to escape their tombs and graves.

The Draugr often spend their time protecting the treasure in their graves from looters or seeking out those who wronged them in their lives. All the Draugr will walk the earth at once, come the day of Ragnarok.

Fenrir

Fenrir is a giant wolf and is one of Loki's children. He is known to be one of the fiercest and most vicious monsters of the nine realms. Many stories told of Fenrir say that he would continue to grow in size and strength, and that nothing could stop him from growing. The gods heard these tales of his size and strength and decided that they needed to chain him so he could not harm anyone.

The gods tried to chain Fenrir many times with strong chains, but he broke through them with ease. Fenrir took this as a game or a challenge of his strength, so when the gods brought a new chain fashioned by the dwarves, he was happy to let them chain him with it. We will discuss this story in detail in the next chapter!

Fenrir plays perhaps one of the most important roles on the day of Ragnarok, as he will be the eventual end to Odin.

Kraken

The Kraken is seen in many different mythologies and it does not solely belong to Norse mythology. What kind of creature the Kraken is, is unclear. Some think it to be a giant squid or octopus while others think it is a giant crab. No matter the type of creature it is, the Kraken is always depicted as being enormous.

The Kraken lives in the deep dark waters of the ocean and it only surfaces if it is disturbed by passing boats. When the Kraken reaches the surface, it is so large that it is often mistaken for an island by sailors. They would sail to it seeking land, only to be pulled down to the depths of the ocean.

Fossegrim

Fossegrim can fit into both the group of creatures and the group of monsters. It is a water spirit that plays music on the violin. It is said that sometimes the spirit will teach others how to play such music, but he requires a goat sacrifice. If the sacrifice is sufficient enough, he will teach them how to play beautiful music, but if it is not, he will only teach them the tune on the fiddle.

Other tales of the Fossegrim say that it will sometimes lure women and children to the lakes, rivers, and streams, and then it will drag them down until they drown. For these reasons, it's easy to see how this can be considered both a humble creature of the realms and a monster.

Jormungandr

The Jormungandr, although a ferocious monster, plays an important role in the protection of both Midgard and humans.

Jormungandr is the name given to the Midgard serpent that lives in the impassable oceans surrounding Midgard. The serpent is said to be so large that its body encircles the world entirely, and it is even able to bite down on its own tail.

Jormungandr is also another child of Loki. Odin tossed the serpent into the sea when it was a small baby, and it was in this ocean that it grew so large. Jormungandr protects Midgard, but not willingly. When the day of Ragnarok comes, it will begin with Jormungandr leaping up from the oceans to poison the sky.

Jormungandr is the sworn enemy of Thor, and they will cause each other's destruction come Ragnarok.

Garmr

Garmr is a blood-stained hellhound that guards the border of Helheim. It lives in a cave called Gnipahellir. The hound is said to be one of the largest, aside from Fenrir, and he always appears with his fur covered in blood. It is unclear where Garmr came from or who he belongs to. He will play a role in Ragnarok, killing many gods and in turn being killed by a god himself.

Hraesvelgr

Hraesvelgr was a giant that wore a large fur coat, and who sits at the north-most part of the universe. His arms turned into giant wings and when he waved them, strong winds would blow over the world. His name means "corpse swallower". He too will play a role in Ragnarok.

Fafnir

He is the son of Hreidmar, the dwarf king, and he was cursed by the treasure that belonged to his father. This curse drove Fafnir crazy with greed, and that greed consumed him. He killed his father in order to obtain his treasure and that treasure went on to curse him even further. It turned him into a horrible, gruesome dragon. The God, Sigurd, eventually slew this dragon and put an end to Fafnir's curse.

Skoll and Hati

These wolves are just a few in the long list of monstrous wolves and hounds in Norse mythology. However, you could argue that they play the most important role out of all the wolves, aside from Fenrir.

Skoll and Hati are large wolves that live in the sky. They each chase after the moon and the sun in the never-ending journey across the sky. Hati chases after the moon, which is represented by the god, Mani, and his brother, Skoll, chases the sun represented by the goddess, Sol.

It is believed that Fenrir was the father of Skoll and Hati, though it is unclear if this is true. What is true is that these two wolves will eventually catch the sun and the moon and devour them whole. This will be one of the many events of Ragnarok that brings about the end of days.

Lyngbakr

This is the largest whale to live in the ocean. It is said that Lyngbakr is so large that it can swallow entire ships whole. Lyngbakr is perhaps the inspiration for stories such as Moby Dick. Unlike most creatures and monsters of the nine realms, the Lyngbakr will play no role in Ragnarok.

Hafgufa

This is yet another sea monster. She is special because she is believed to be the mother of all other sea monsters. In most stories, she is said to be a colossal fish that looks more like an island. She feeds on ships, whales, sometimes men, and anything else she can catch.

Nidhogg

Nidhogg's importance in the existence of life and its inevitable end cannot be overstated.

Nidhogg is a primordial dragon known as "the devourer" who lives at the base of the world tree, Yggdrasil. Nidhogg is constantly gnawing away at one of the three roots of the world tree that lies in Niflheim. It is said that come the time of Ragnarok, Nidhogg will have finally chewed through the root of the world tree, throwing it and the whole universe out of balance.

Nidhogg will destroy the world tree and throw everything back into the chaos it was born from.

Giants

There are many different giants that live in two different realms. All giants are known as evil, destructive, and chaotic forces. The fire giants live in Muspellheim, a realm of fire and smoke. The frost giants and rock giants live in Jotunheim, and they are the sworn enemy of the Aesir and Vanir gods.

The giants and the gods are in a constant battle. The gods want to create order in the universe and the giants want to throw it back into the chaos it came from. Their constant struggle is symbolic of the cycle of life. All things that are created from chaos come into order, but everything must return to chaos at some point. The giants play one of the biggest roles in Norse mythology.

Surtr

Surtr is an enormous primordial giant that rules over the realm of Muspellheim. He is the sworn enemy of the Aesir gods, and he waits in his realm for the chance to destroy Asgard and bring an end to the rule of the Aesir gods.

Come the day of Ragnorok, Garmr will let out a blood-curdling howl and this will act as a signal to Surtr. He will grab his large, flaming sword and ride from his realm to Asgard. He will level the realm and burn it to the ground. Then, he will lead the fire giants to the final battle.

Chapter 4: A Hero's Tale

Norse mythology is surrounded by great tales of heroes' ventures across the nine realms. Tales speak of great battles won and lost by the gods. These tales were more than just bedtime stories or scary tales told by the fireside to the Norse. They played an important role in their culture. Nothing in Norse mythology was ever unimportant or useless. Every tale, whether the hero won or lost, provided knowledge and a way to see the world.

The Building of Asgard's Wall

Asgard is known as the stronghold of the gods for a reason. The wall around their stronghold is known to withstand any attack from the enemies of the gods. This wall is what protects the gods and what makes Asgard such an impenetrable stronghold. This wall was not always there. The tale of how this wall came to be is a grand one filled with deceit and cunning.

At the start of the world, when Asgard was first built and still new, a smith in disguise came to the gods with a proposition. The gods knew how open and defenseless they were to any attack from their many enemies, and so this smith offered to build them a wall that could withstand any attack. The smith said that he could do this in just three seasons, but his price was steep. He would build the wall for the gods but, he asked for the Goddess Freya's hand in marriage and to take the sun and the moon as his own.

The gods laughed at the smith for making such bold claims, but they sent him away so they could take council on it. They needed a wall that was strong enough to hold against the giants, and this smith was promising them just that. At this point, Loki suggested they give the smith what he asks for: Freya, the moon, and the sun, but on the condition that he completes the wall in a single winter.

The Gods had no intention of giving the smith any of these things, but they knew the task was an impossible one, so they agreed to Loki's plan. The smith agreed to their terms as long as his horse could help, and he made all the Gods swear to keep their side of the deal when he completes the wall.

The gods laughed to themselves as the smith got to work on the wall. They knew that he couldn't complete the wall in just one winter, even with the help of his horse. They would get at least part of a wall and the smith would receive nothing. However, to the shock of the Gods, the smith made quick work of the wall.

To their surprise, the smith's horse, Svadilfari, was doing twice as much work as the smith. It dragged large boulders back and forth all day and night while the smith picked the large boulders up and put them into place himself. The Gods started to suspect they were being deceived. There was no way that a man of the smith's size could lift such large boulders, and his horse was not just a regular horse at all.

The Gods turned their anger to Loki, for he had convinced them to agree to this plan. The end of winter was but three days away and the great wall was not far from being complete. Only a few boulders by the gate needed to be placed. The Gods threatened Loki with death if he did not put things right.

The night before the completion of the wall, the smith and his horse were out in the forest collecting the final boulders they needed. Suddenly, a mare who was none other than Loki in disguise appeared and excited the smith's horse. Svadilfari broke his reins and chased after the mare. The smith ran after his horse but Svadilfari was too fast to catch.

The smith looked for his horse all night and when the sun began to rise on the last day of winter, he knew that he could not complete the wall in time. The smith broke out in anger. He knew that the gods had tricked him. It was them who had sent a mare to steal away his horse on the final night of winter. In the middle of the smith's anger, his disguise fell away and the Gods watched in horror as a large monstrous giant stood in the smith's place.

Thor was quick to call his hammer, Mjollnir, and attack the giant. The giant raised his hands to destroy the wall he had built for the gods, but Thor slammed his hammer into the giant's head, smashing his skull to pieces and slaying him on the spot.

Loki was missing for several days and he returned one night with Sleipnir, an eight-legged horse, as a gift for Odin. The Gods forgave Loki and welcomed him back into Asgard. Odin took Loki's gift happily, and Sleipnir grew up to become the fastest steed in the nine realms.

Odin's Discovery of the Runes

Odin, the All-Father, is one of the wisest gods and this is because he has spent almost all of his life in a relentless pursuit of knowledge. One of the tales that show off Odin's strong will and need for absolute knowledge and wisdom is the tale of when he discovered the runes.

The runes were more than just a language. Those who understood them could understand the mysteries of the universe and life itself. The runes would allow one to interact with, access, and influence how the world is shaped. This is why Odin sought their knowledge.

The world tree, Yggdrasil, grows strong and tall in the center of the universe, holding up all of the nine realms. One of its three roots feeds directly from the Well of Urd. The Norns, three mystical and powerful women, care for the roots and stay by the Well of Urda. The Norns know the runes and they use them to control the fate of lives around the nine realms. Odin sat in his high throne in Asgard and watched them do this. He was envious of their power and wisdom. He longed to know the secret of the runes, and nothing would stop him in this pursuit.

The Well of Urda requires a sacrifice significant enough to obtain the knowledge it holds. Odin hung himself from Yggdrasil's branch with his spear pierced through his chest and the branch. Odin peered down into the dark, bottomless waters of the well. Odin hung himself in this position and accepted no help from any of the gods. He would not even accept a sip of water. The Well of Urda required him to prove himself worthy of the knowledge of the runes, and so Odin would do that.

Odin stayed like this for no less than nine days and nine nights, staring down into the ever-circling waters. He was on the edge, tethering between the land of the living and the land of the dead. Finally, on the ninth night, Odin saw shapes take form in the water. The runes had finally revealed themselves to him. Odin had proved himself worthy of their knowledge. Odin needed only to see them once, and their knowledge was burned into his memory.

Odin ended his nine days and nine nights with a scream of exultation. Because of his sacrifice, Odin became one of the wisest and mightiest gods in the nine realms.

The Binding of Fenrir

The sly and mischievous god, Loki, had many children in his time. Each of his children were either monstrous in form and shape, or they were mere creatures with fantastic talents and skill. Loki's most famous children were the three hideous ones he fathered with the giantess, Angrboda.

The first of their children was Jormungand, the Midgard serpent, the second was Hel, the goddess of the dead, and the third of their children was the great wolf, Fenrir. The gods had terrible visions of death and destruction being caused by these three children and they sought to make sure this would never happen.

Odin took Jormungand, a small, snake-sized serpent at the time, and threw him into the ocean around Midgard. He continued to grow and soon became so large that he could encircle Midgard entirely. They banished Hel to the underworld for her face resembled those of the decaying dead, and she soon became a goddess of her own realm named Helheim. Fenrir inspired so much fear in the gods' hearts that they dared not let him out of their sights. They raised him themselves in their stronghold, Asgard, and only Tyr was brave enough to feed him.

The gods watched Fenrir every day, and their fears only grew stronger as Fenrir continued to grow larger. Fenrir grew at such an alarming rate that the gods knew he could not stay in Asgard for much longer. They knew what kind of death and destruction

Fenrir would leave in his wake if he were allowed to roam free, and so they decided to bind him.

The gods gained the wolf's trust by telling him they wanted to test his strength. They would bind him in chains and each time Fenrir broke through the chains, they would pretend to cheer and clap for him. Fenrir grinned and welcomed the challenge. He called for them to bind him again and again, and he broke every chain they used to bind him.

The gods weren't sure what they could do. Fenrir kept increasing in size and strength. They called for the dwarves to make them a chain so strong that Fenrir would never be able to break free. The dwarves made them a chain called Gleipnir, which was as thin as a silk ribbon.

When the gods presented this chain to Fenrir, he was untrusting of them. He refused to let them chain him, knowing that they were trying to trick him. The gods were cunning and chose to stroke his ego. They told him that there was no chain in existence that he could not break for he was the strongest creature alive. Fenrir smiled, for he knew that this was true. He agreed to let them chain him with Gleipnir, but under the condition that one of the gods held their hand in between his open jaws. If he could not break free of the chain, he would bite down on the god's hand.

None of the Gods wanted to agree to this, for they did not want to lose their hand or break an oath. Tyr, the bravest of all the

Gods, stepped forward and agreed to do as Fenrir asked. Fenrir opened his mouth wide and Tyr held his hand out in the wolf's mouth. The Gods worked quickly to wrap the chain around Fenrir and bind him tight.

When they were done, they all stepped away and watched Fenrir squirm as he tried to break free. Although the chain was thin as a silk ribbon, Fenrir could not break free of it. When he realized what the gods had done, he snapped his jaw down on Tyr's arm and swallowed it whole.

Tyr cried out in pain, but he smiled because he had done his job well. The great wolf was bound, and he could cause no harm to anyone. The Gods carried Fenrir to a dark and isolated place and wrapped his chain around a boulder. Odin stuck a sword in between Fenrir's open jaws so that he would never be able to close his mouth again. They left Fenrir there, where he howled and growled ceaselessly until Ragnarok.

The Death of Baldur

Out of all the gods, Baldur was the most beloved. He is the son of Odin and Frigg. He is joyful, generous, and courageous. He lifted the spirits and gladdened the hearts of all with his presence. Out of all those who love him, no one loved him more than his mother.

Baldur struggled to sleep. He spent many nights having dreams of misfortune befalling him and death finally catching up with him. All the gods turned to Odin to discover the meaning of these dreams. Odin, the wisest of all, wasted no time in discovering that these dreams were telling of Baldur's coming demise.

The gods mourned for there was now nothing they could do to save their beloved Baldur. Frigg, who loved her son more than anything, would not stand idly by while death crept up on Baldur. She was a sorceress after all, and she would use her magic to save him.

Frigg went out into the universe and visited each of the nine realms. She went to every being, living or not, and obtained oaths from each of them that they would do no harm to Baldur. These oaths were all secure, and so Baldur became immortal as nothing in the cosmos could harm him.

The gods soon turned this into a game. They each took turns throwing whatever weapon they had at Baldur while he stood there proudly as each attack bounced off of him with ease. Nothing and no one could harm him. The sly and disloyal God, Loki, sensed an opportunity for mischief and revenge.

Loki disguised himself as an old and frail woman and went to Frigg in the night. He asked her, "Did all things truly swear an oath to do no harm to Baldur?"

"Oh, yes!" Frigg replied but she hesitated for a moment. "Well, everything except for the mistletoe, but it is so small and harmless. What harm could it do to my son?"

Frigg saw no harm in telling the old woman this, but as soon as the news hit Loki's ears, he departed. He put his plans into place and set up his revenge. He would see Odin suffer at losing his children just how he had suffered by losing his.

Loki sought out the only bush in Asgard where mistletoe grew, and he carved a spear out of the wood. He kept that spear hidden and brought it with him to the game that the gods loved to play the most.

Baldur stood proud and tall as the gods took turns throwing their weapons at him. Loki knew that he could not join in on the game himself or the gods would instantly suspect him of something. He scanned the room and spotted Hodr, the blind god, standing in the corner by himself. Loki grinned and approached the blind god.

"Do you not feel left out?" Loki asked Hodr. "All the gods join in on the game and you cannot."

"There is nothing I can do about it," the blind god replied, "If I throw a weapon at him, I would only miss and be laughed at."

Loki paused for a moment and then faked a gasp, "I have an idea! Here, take this," Loki placed the spear made of mistletoe in the blind gods hand, "I will point your hand in the direction of where

Baldur stands, and then all you have to do is toss this spear at him."

Hodr smiled and thanked Loki for caring to help him. Loki tried his hardest not to smile as he led Hodr to the front of the room and aimed the spear for him. Baldur stood proudly for the last time as the blind god tossed the spear towards him.

The spear flew through the air and everyone stared in horror as it pierced Baldur straight through, and his body dropped to the floor, limp and lifeless.

Loki left before the gods were able to compose themselves. No one could believe that Baldur was truly dead. They mourned the loss of their beloved god and also feared the events that were to follow it, for they were all aware that this was but the first sign of the end of days and the final battle to come.

The gods arranged a grand funeral for Baldur while the God, Hermod, rode on the back of Sleipner to the gates of Hel. It was a long journey, but he finally made it to the underworld, where he begged at the Goddess Hel's feet for her to release Baldur from her realm.

Hel smiled and denied his request. A son of Odin was quite the prize and she intended to keep Baldur there for all eternity. He would never feel the sun on his face nor see the light of day again. Never again would his joyful and graceful soul gladden the hearts of others.

The End

Since the beginning of time, the gods and goddesses have feared the day of Ragnarok. It is the day that will end everything that lives and throw the ordered world they have created back into chaos. The great world tree, Yggdrasil, will not be able to escape the end of days. No matter how long the gods spend preparing for Ragnarok and no matter how much knowledge Odin gathers, no one knows when the day that will end all days will come. All they can do is wait until they see the signs that have been prophesized.

All gods know the signs of Ragnarok, and all fear the day that the first sign will appear.

The gods and goddesses experienced the worst winter of their time, that dragged on for three years. It was the coldest and harshest winter to ever come to them, and also the longest. It seemed as though this winter would never come to an end.

After three long years with no sun or warmth in between, the gods knew what this winter meant. Odin sat upon his throne in his high hall with his wolves by his feet and his ravens on his shoulders. He did not need their whispers or their eyes to know what it meant. This winter was but the first sign of Ragnarok.

Odin knew that the legends and myths of Ragnarok all spoke of a long never-ending winter being the first sign, but he knew deep in his heart that the death of his son, Baldur, was actually the first sign. He was still morning the loss of his beloved son and even though he got revenge on his murderer, Loki, it still seemed like a wound in his heart that would never heal.

The gods and goddesses did not believe Odin when he spoke that such events are signs of the end of days. The final battle was coming, and Odin knew it. There were more signs of this spread across the nine realms. Odin knew of these signs because they had been seen by is ravens and this knowledge had been whispered into his ear.

War had broken out in all of the nine realms and it appeared that people were fighting for no reason at all. These wars closely resembled a spreading plague and the only explanation that Odin could think of was the coming of Ragnarok.

Odin leaned back in his chair and drank from his golden goblet of red wine while his ravens, Huginn and Munin, whispered the events of the day in his ear. He heard of many wars, but he did not care much for this knowledge. Huginn spoke briefly of a red rooster that had visited Jotunheim, the land of the giants, in Odin's ear. In the other ear, Munin spoke of a second red rooster that visited the Goddess of Hel in Helheim at the exact same time as the first rooster.

Odin gasped and loosened his grip on his golden goblet. The goblet fell to the ground, his wolves leaping out of its way as the red wine splashed out, drenching the golden floor.

The silence of the day was broken by the cry of a black rooster with a golden comb named Gullinkambi, who had come to visit the gods in Asgard. Odin stood up as he heard the crow of the black rooster. The red wine from his goblet ran down the stairs leading to his throne and flowed across the floor. It resembled a river of blood flowing through Hel's gates. As Freki, his wolf, lapped up the wine from the floor, an image of a great wolf drinking from the river of blood flashed past his eyes. There was no doubt in Odin's mind. Ragnarok was upon them.

Odin grabbed his spear fashioned for him by the dwarves and rushed from his hall. He had determination in his eye and red wine in his beard. He would warn everyone of the coming end, but as he walked out of those doors, the sky was filled with a thundering sound. Heimdall saw the signs not a moment too soon and blew on his horn to warn everyone. The sound travelled throughout the nine realms and straight to the heart of Asgard where the Hall of Valhalla stood.

The warriors, fallen in battle and chosen by Odin himself to fight in the last battle, heard Heimdall's horn and acted quickly. The warriors prepared themselves and marched from the gates of Valhalla. Their armor was polished and each one was studded with jewels and gold. They held their weapons at the ready. Each arrow, dagger, spear, and sword was sharpened and ready for battle.

Odin saw his warriors gathering and marching towards the Bifrost. They were ready, but he was not yet sure if they needed to go to battle. Odin made his way to the Bifrost himself for he needed more than the whispers of his ravens to confirm the signs. He needed Heimdall's eyes to tell him if it was true.

"Heimdall, tell me, what do you see!" Odin's thundering voice bellowed as he marched towards Heimdall.

Heimdall turned his all-seeing eyes to the skies. From his place beside the Bifrost, he could look into all nine realms.

"The giants are marching. They bare weapons and armor. They march as if they are marching to war." Heimdall replied to his king's question.

"Get everyone behind the wall!" Odin ordered as he began to walk back to his hall to prepare for battle. "If they want a war, then it is a war they will get."

"They are not marching towards Asgard, All-Father," Heimdall called to Odin before he could make his way to his hall. "They are headed in the opposite direction. They are marching down to Helheim."

"What?" Odin whispered to himself. "Why would they be going there?"

Heimdall did not answer the question for he knew it was not directed at him. Odin was deep inside his own mind, trying to find answers to this puzzle. He did not hear the urgent footsteps coming towards him nor the voice of his son, Thor, calling out to him.

"Father!" Thor cried out. "It's Baldur, he's back. Father, Baldur is back."

Odin heard the name of his dead son for whom he had already grieved, and he was pulled from his thoughts. Odin looked to see the face of his beloved son standing in front of him. Odin could not contain his joy. He threw his arms around Baldur and pulled him in tight for a hug.

"How is this possible?" Odin muttered, tears filling his eyes. "This must be some trick! There is no way that Hel would have released you without some kind of gift or trade."

"It is not a trick, father," Baldur assured Odin. "It is really me. I'm here, but I bring with me the most terrible news."

Odin released his son from his grasp and wiped the tears from his face. He stared into his son's eyes and gave him a nod.

"Tell me your news, son."

"It is not just I that Hel has released," Baldur explained. "Helheim is empty, and the gates are wide open. She has released everyone from Hel, and they march with her to war. They say it will be the war to end all wars."

Odin's face became still and emotionless, but one eye was filled with dread.

"They march to Ragnarok." He whispered. "Then, we will march to meet them!"

Odin walked to his hall while his sons, Thor and Baldur, split and spread throughout Asgard. They warned all the gods and goddesses of the coming war. They all prepared for war, and across the rainbow bridge, the gods and goddesses rode to meet their enemies in the final battle.

Sleipnir carried Odin far ahead of the others, but he did not slow down nor stop to wait for them. The battle was waiting for him. As they rode down towards Hel, a great shadow appeared in the sky above them.

The shadow in the sky grew ever darker and took the form of a wolf on the moon's surface. Skoll opened his mouth wide and swallowed the moon whole, along with the god, Mani. All light in the sky disappeared down the wolf's throat. There was no doubt in Odin's mind that Hati has surely devoured Sol along with her sun. Complete darkness fell over the nine realms as they rode to Ragnarok.

This was the third sign of Ragnarok, but Odin could pay it no further attention. He put his mind back on the road ahead and the battle to come.

As the gods and goddesses rode down the Bifrost to the underworld, Hel stood at the helm of her ship and watched all manner of creatures get on board. Giants from Jotunheim and the undead from her realm all boarded the ship as one, but she was surprised to see one person in particular boarding her ship.

Hel walked down from her helm in order to meet him as he boarded her ship.

"I am surprised to see you here, father." Hel spoke.

Loki walked onto the ship with Fenrir walking beside him. Fenrir had grown so large he was almost the same size as Hel herself.

"Where else did you think I would be?" Loki asked Hel.

"Is it not your way to always run back to Odin, kissing the ground at his feet and begging to stand by his side once more?"

Loki sneered and glanced to the wolf by his side. "Not this time."

Hel stepped aside as Loki and Fenrir pushed passed her and boarded the ship. She returned to her place at the helm as the bulk of the giant army arrived. Once they were all boarded, the ship set sail. She glanced down at the army of monsters, giants, and the undead below her.

"This will be a great battle." She whispered.

The final battle raged on. Many warriors were struck down on both sides and Odin watched in horror as the Aesir fell one by one around him. The giants were formidable foes, but Odin knocked them down with ease. Odin slashed through one enemy after the other and the ground began to shake beneath him.

Odin turned, expecting to see an army marching towards him. Instead, he saw only one enemy. The great Fenrir galloped towards him, his jaw still stuck wide open with the sword that Odin put in his mouth. During his captivity, Fenrir's growth was only slowed, but not stopped. He was now larger than the great wolves of the sky, Hati and Skoll.

The wolf dragged his open jaw along the ground as he ran straight towards Odin. He swallowed up anyone unfortunate enough to get in his way. Fenrir was on no one's side in this battle. He swallowed both giant and god that got in his way. His only goal was revenge on Odin for imprisoning him.

Odin lifted his spear in the air and threw it at the great wolf. The spear never missed its mark and its aim was true. It struck Fenrir in the side and the wolf let out a screeching howl, staggering back from the force of the impact. Odin was without a weapon now and the enemies around him took advantage of this.

Thor and Tyr rushed to Odin's aid, striking down the enemies surrounding him and protecting the All-Father from harm. Odin made his way across the battlefield towards Fenrir to finished him. Thor and Tyr moved with him, knocking giants and the undead out of his way and clearing a path towards Fenrir.

Tyr was knocked off his feet by Garmr, the blood wolf that guards the gates of Hel, and so Thor was left alone to defend Odin. Thor was nearly overwhelmed, but Odin picked up a sword and joined him in the fight with his eye still fixed on Fenrir. Thor was knocked off his feet and by the time he got back up, he lost sight of the All-Father, but a new sight stole his attention.

The ground shook and the waves crashed onto the shore as the great Midgard Serpent burst through the surface of the water. The serpent opened its mouth wide and spat its hot venom all over the battlefield, killing anything in its path and burning the ground. Thor gripped the handle of Mjollnir tightly and glared up at the serpent.

Thor spun his hammer round and round in circles, gathering all the force and energy that he could. All at once, he let loose the power and the hammer shot up towards the Midgard Serpent. Thor surprised the serpent and slammed into the bottom of his jaw. The serpents jaw slammed shut, biting off its own tongue. Thor fell back to the ground and landed, cracking the floor round him.

The serpent gave Thor no time to recover. It opened its jaw wide and shot down towards Thor. He didn't react fast enough to jump out of the way. Instead, Thor threw his arms out to his side as the serpent's jaw closed around him. Thor pushed the serpent's mouth open with all his might as it threatened to snap shut and swallow him whole. He cried out in pain as its teeth tore through the skin of his arm.

Thor felt weak as the venom burned through his body. With the last bit of strength that he had left, he forced the serpent's mouth open further, tearing his top jaw free of his lower jaw. Thor ripped the top of the serpent's mouth clean off, and through it into the ocean. The serpent's body sunk to the bottom of the ocean as Thor fell limp and lifeless to the ground as the venom burnt through him. No god or goddesses, no matter how mighty, could survive the Midgard serpent's venom.

Meanwhile, Odin continued across the battlefield towards Fenrir. He grabbed the spear protruding from the wolf's side and Fenrir let out a cry as Odin pulled it free. He raised it high above the wolf's skull and forced it down. Odin struck his spear in the hard place between the Fenrir's eyes, but his skull was so thick that Odin could not push his spear deep enough to kill him.

Fenrir cried out and shook his head, knocking Odin back to the ground. Fenrir was so angry that he forced his jaw closed, bending the sword that was holding it open. Fenrir bared his teeth at Odin, testing the new freedom of his jaw. He shook his head again to get rid of Odin's spear, but the spear was so deep that he couldn't shake it free.

Odin tried to get up off the ground, but he couldn't find the strength to do so. The world around him spun and the ground beneath him shook. The last thing he saw was the back of Fenrir's throat as he was swallowed whole.

The battle continued to rage on the plains of Vigrid. The ground was soaked in blood and dead bodies were scattered around. God slew giant and giant slew god. Loki and Heimdall engaged in a fatal knife fight, cutting each other and each dying of their wounds. Tyr killed the bloodhound, Gramr, and then died of the wounds the wolf of Hel had given him.

As the final battle continued, one giant did not think to join it. Instead, Surtr, the king fire Giant of Muspellheim, raised his large, flaming sword and rode for Asgard. He set the stronghold of the giants alight and watched it burn to the ground. One by one, Surtr rode to each of the nine realms, setting them ablaze like his own realm and breathing in the smoke and the sparks. He set the sky on fire and watched the whole world burn.

The world tree, Yggdrasil, could no longer hole up the nine realms and it began to shake and lean. After years of gnawing at the root, Nidhogg finally broke through, separating Yggdrasil from one of its roots. Yggdrasil shook while all of the nine realms burned. Ash rose into the air and all gods and giants burned in the fire that Surtr had set.

Yggdrasil shook and leaned, but it did not fall. The world tree stood tall as everything burned around it. It was foretold that all will burn before the battle ends. From the ash of the old world, a new one shall rise for not everything has perished in the end. Before the battle began, a single man named Liftraser and a woman called Lif saw the signs of Ragnarok and took refuge inside Yggdrasil. They came out when the battle had ended and when all was gone.

A new world rose from the sea and the man and woman called this their new home. They continued to live and prosper, and they will became the ancestors for the new line of mankind.

Not all the gods perished in the final days. Those who survived traveled to a paradise named Idavoll, that was untouched by the events of Ragnarok. This is where they made their new lives and built their new homes. This is where the gods would try to return to their life of order and peace. The gods live here, but they live in fear.

Nidhogg survived the final days of Ragnarok and he made a new home for himself in the underworld. The gods could see his shadow as he flew through the sky past the new moon, carrying the bodies of those who died in the final battle. He took them to his home and feasts on them while he waits for the next war to rage.

This is the story of Ragnarok, the end of everything, even the gods.

www.ingramcontent.com/pod-product-compliance
Lightning Source LLC
LaVergne TN
LVHW011740060526
838200LV00051B/3272